Paleo Freezer

Delicious, Fix & Freeze, Gluten-Free, Paleo Recipes for Busy People

Lucy Fast

Disclaimer and Terms of Use: The Author and Publisher has strived to be as accurate and complete as possible in the creation of this book, notwithstanding the fact that she does not warrant or represent at any time that the contents within are accurate due to the rapidly changing nature of the Internet. While all attempts have been made to verify information provided in this publication, the Author and Publisher assumes no responsibility for errors, omissions, or contrary interpretation of the subject matter herein. Any perceived slights of specific persons, peoples, or organizations are unintentional. In practical advice books, like anything else in life, there are no guarantees of income made. This book is not intended for use as a source of legal, business, accounting or financial advice. All readers are advised to seek services of competent professionals in legal, business, accounting, and finance field.

Printed in the United States of America

Just to say Thank You for Purchasing this Book I want to give you a gift <u>100% absolutely FREE</u>

A Copy of My Upcoming Special Report

"Paleo Pantry: The Beginner's Guide to What Should and Should NOT be in Your Paleo Kitchen"

Go to <u>www.aPaleoPantry.com</u> to Reserve Your FREE Copy

Table of Contents

INTRODUCTION **5**

SAFE AND EASY FREEZER STORAGE **6**

WINNER WINNER CHICKEN DINNERS! **8**

Chicken Wrap 8
Chicken with Vegetables and Coconut Milk 11
Vegetables and Chicken Wok 13
Chicken Curry 15
Oven Cooked Chicken with Herbs 17
Chicken with Almonds and Mango 19

PALEO PEOPLE EAT *MEAT* DINNERS **21**

Grilled Lamb Brochette with Mediterranean Salad 21
Tenderloin Casserole with White Wine and Baked Vegetables 24
Meat Balls 26
Wild Game Stew 29
Liver and Onions 32
Lamb Casserole 34

DINING ON THE COASTS - SEAFOOD DINNERS **37**

Mussels Provencal 37
Sautéed Shrimp with Asparagus 40
Galician Octopus 42
Baked Fish 45
Tuna Salad 47
Garlic Shrimp 49

VEGGIE DINNERS AND SIDES **51**

Mushrooms Provencal 51
Scrambled Zucchini 53
Zucchini Omelets and Tomato Salad 55
Stuffed Avocado 57
Spinach with Coconut and Spices 59
Artichoke Omelets 61

CONCLUSION **63**

CHECK OUT THE OTHER YUMMY BOOKS IN MY PALEO DIET SOLUTION SERIES!! **64**

Introduction

I want to thank you and congratulate you for purchasing ***Paleo Freezer: Delicious, Fix & Freeze, Gluten-Free, Paleo Recipes for Busy People***.

This book contains proven steps and strategies making eating a variety of Paleo dinners a whole lot easier. This book will take you on a culinary journey through poultry, meat, seafood and vegetable dinner dishes that are made with whole, nutritious and delicious ingredients.

Each recipe includes directions to make the dinner, freeze it, reheat it and then make it in bulk if you really like it. Plan ahead and make dinner time a breeze by simply reheating impressive and flavorful dishes. Your family will think you brought home take out from a fine dining restaurant.

Thanks again for purchasing this book, I hope you enjoy it!

Lucy Fast

Safe and Easy Freezer Storage

There are a few things that are good to know when you are storing food in the freezer.

1. You will need large Ziploc freezer bags and/or Tupperware.

2. It is important to allow the dishes to cool after initially preparing them BEFORE storing them for freezing.

3. You can freeze almost any kind of food safely with the exception of eggs in their shells and canned foods.

4. Some foods do not freeze very well including lettuce, creamy sauces and mayonnaise.

5. The best foods to freeze are meat, poultry and seafood, as they maintain their quality well.

Let's get a little scientific here. By freezing your food, you are preventing the growth of microorganisms that cause food to spoil. This is a great news for busy people who want to prepare ahead to make for a convenient, quality dinner time.

There is more good news for freezing foods. Although yeasts, molds and bacteria are inactivated, the freshness and nutrients remain intact through the freezing process. All the good vitamins and minerals present in these Paleo recipes, will be available despite the freezer.

Freezer burn is a common problem that can be avoided with proper storage. It is caused by the skin of food coming in contact with the freezer air. The food is not unsafe but turns a grayish color and should be discarded. If your food is purchased in a vacuum sealed bag, you can freeze it that way. If it is just a plastic wrap, you may want to wrap it again to be safe. All of the meals you prepare throughout this book should be stored in a sealable plastic bag or Tupperware container.

Freezing foods at 0 degrees Fahrenheit keeps them safe pretty much indefinitely but the quality does decrease in time. For that reason, we have recommended storage times of about 4 months (it will be specified in the recipe). Once you are ready to cook the food, it is again vulnerable to deterioration and microorganisms once thawed. Thawing must be done according to the directions in order to maintain safety.

Take advantage of these meals made in advance and literally freeze them in time until you are ready to enjoy them!

Winner Winner Chicken Dinners!

Chicken Wrap

Makes one meal for a family of four

Ingredients:

- 1 head of lettuce (purchase when you are going to defrost and serve this dish to ensure freshness.)
- 2 lbs. of chicken
- 2 medium onions diced small
- 2 medium eggplants diced 0small
- 1 red pepper diced small
- 8 ounces mushrooms diced small
- 2 zucchinis
- Half a glass of white wine
- Oregano, sea salt, freshly ground black pepper to taste
- Extra virgin olive oil
- Sesame Seeds (optional)

Preparation Instructions:

1. In a skillet, add olive oil, onions and red pepper, cooking until onions is transparent on medium high heat
2. Add the chicken and cook for about 6 minutes more
3. Add the eggplant, zucchini, and mushrooms
4. Cook another five minutes and then add the wine and raise the heat to reduce the mixture.
5. Sprinkle with oregano and add a splash of oil
6. Let simmer 2 minutes more and turn off the heat
7. For serving, Wash the lettuce and separate the leaves, reserving the largest leaves to use as a wrap. Place the stuffing inside each lettuce leaf, garnish with Sesame Seeds and wrap.

Freezing Instructions:
Freeze in zip lock freezer bags or Tupperware for up to four months. Be sure and keep labels on hand so you can put the freeze date.

Make this meal in bulk:
Makes three meals for a family of four

Ingredients measurements:

- 3 heads of lettuce (Buy the lettuce within 2 days of serving.)
- 6 lbs. of chicken
- 6 medium onions diced small
- 6 medium eggplants diced small
- 3 red peppers diced small
- 1 ½ lbs. mushrooms diced small
- 6 zucchinis
- One and a half a glass of white wine

- Oregano, sea salt, freshly ground black pepper to taste
- Extra virgin olive oil

Differences in Prep:
Use a bigger pot vs. a pan (if you have one) or separate it and cook it in three portions.

Chicken with Vegetables and Coconut Milk

Makes one meal for a family of four

Ingredients:

- 4 carrots boiled or grilled and sliced
- Coconut oil
- Coconut milk
- 2 lbs. chicken breast cut into cubes
- 2 large leeks, cut into strips
- Pinch of sea salt
- Cayenne pepper

Preparation Instructions:

1. Put a little coconut oil in a pan, heat, and then add the cubed chicken cubes and cook until browned
2. Add leeks, stirring occasionally
3. When the leeks are soft, incorporate the boiled carrot slices and a splash of coconut milk
4. Season with a little sea salt and cayenne pepper to taste

Freezing Instructions:

Freeze in zip lock freezer bags or Tupperware for up to four months. Be sure and keep labels on hand so you can put the freeze date.

Cooking Directions:

Take meal out of the freezer the night before and leave it in the refrigerator all night. If not completely thawed by dinner time, take it out and let sit at room temperature for a little while. Reheat in pan, the same way you cooked it the first time.

Make this meal in bulk:
Makes three meals for a family of four

Ingredients:

- 12 carrots boiled or grilled and sliced
- Coconut oil, enough to sauté the chicken and veggies
- Coconut milk, 3 splashes
- 6 lbs. chicken breast cut into cubes
- 6 large leeks, cut into strips
- 3 pinches of sea salt
- Cayenne pepper to taste

Differences in Prep:
Use a bigger pot vs. a pan (if you have one) or separate it and cook it in three portions.

Vegetables and Chicken Wok

Makes one meal for a family of four

Ingredients:

- 2 lbs. chicken breast cut into strips
- 2 onions
- 8 asparagus, chopped
- 2 red bell peppers
- 2 zucchinis, chopped
- 14 oz. of mushrooms, cut in slices
- 6 cloves of garlic, chopped finely
- Coconut oil
- Half a glass of white wine
- Sea salt to taste
- Turmeric to taste

Preparation Instructions:

1. Cut the onion into eighths and place in wok with a little coconut oil. Add asparagus, pepper and let cook for 5 min. on medium high heat
2. Add chopped zucchini. When everything is soft, add the wine, and raise the heat. When the mixture reduces, turn the fire down again to low
3. In a pan, add garlic and a little oil.
4. Add the Chicken and sauté 6 minutes.
5. Add the vegetables and toss with turmeric. Cook for 2-3 minutes more
6. Serve hot

Freezing Instructions:

Freeze in zip lock freezer bags or Tupperware for up to four months. Be sure and keep labels on hand so you can put the freeze date.

Make this meal in bulk:
Makes three meals for a family of four

Ingredients measurements:

- 6 lbs. chicken breast cut into strips
- 6 onions
- 24 asparagus, chopped
- 6 red bell peppers
- 6 Zucchinis, chopped
- 42 oz. of mushrooms, cut in slices
- 18 cloves of garlic, chopped finely
- Coconut oil
- 1 1/2 a glass of white wine
- Sea salt to taste
- Turmeric to taste

Differences in Prep:
Use a bigger pot vs. a pan (if you have one) or separate it and cook it in three portions.

Chicken Curry

Makes one meal for a family of four

Ingredients:

- 4 chicken breasts, cubed
- 4 carrots, sliced
- 2 onions, cut into eighths
- 2 cups coconut milk
- 2 tsp. curry paste
- 2 tablespoons coconut oil
- ¼ cup ground almonds
- 2 cloves
- 2 small pieces of stick cinnamon
- 2 tsp. turmeric
- 1 finger of freshly ground ginger
- A few curry leaves (fresh or dry, optional)

Preparation Instructions:

1. In a pot add coconut oil, heat, and add the onion, cook for 5 minutes
2. Add carrots and cook for another 5 minutes
3. Add cubed chicken and cook until firm
4. Add curry paste and ground almonds, shredded coconut, cloves, ginger, and curry leaves. Cook for another 5 minutes
5. Now we add the coconut milk (to everyone's taste, depending on how thin you like the sauce)
6. Cook for a few minutes more, stirring occasionally to reduce and blend the in ingredients and flavors
7. Let stand over low heat about 10 to 15 minutes more, so the chicken will finish cooking

Freezing Instructions:
Freeze in zip lock freezer bags or Tupperware for up to four months. Be sure and keep labels on hand so you can put the freeze date.

Cooking Directions:
Take meal out of the freezer the night before and leave it in the refrigerator all night. If not completely thawed by dinnertime take it out and let sit at room temperature for a little while. Reheat in pot, the same way you cooked it the first time.

Make this meal in bulk:
Makes three meals for a family of four

Ingredients measurements:

- 12 chicken breasts, cubed
- 12 carrots, sliced
- 6 onions, cut into eighths
- 6 cups coconut milk
- 6 tsp. curry paste
- 6 tablespoons coconut oil
- ¾ cup ground almonds
- 6 cloves
- 6 small pieces of stick cinnamon
- 6 tsp. turmeric
- 3 finger of freshly ground ginger
- A few curry leaves (fresh or dry, optional)

Differences in Prep:
Use a bigger pot vs. a pan (if you have one) or separate it and cook it in three portions.

Oven Cooked Chicken with Herbs

Makes one meal for a family of four

Ingredients:

- 1 whole chicken
- 1 head of garlic, peel all the cloves, chop coarsely
- 3 lemons, sliced, save a little lemon juice for later
- 1 tablespoon thyme
- 4 tablespoons olive oil
- Sea salt to taste
- Freshly ground black pepper to taste

Preparation Instructions:

1. Preheat oven to 375 F.
2. Clean the chicken, removing the skin and fat
3. Place chicken in a roasting pan with olive oil, season to taste and rub some oil on the chicken with your hands. When the oven is hot, put the chicken in and start cooking it
4. After about 15 minutes, remove the chicken from the oven and add the garlic, thyme, lemon slices, and lemon juice over chicken
5. Put the roasting pan back in the oven and reduce the temperature to 350 F. Let it bake for about 45 minutes, turning it occasionally and basting with the pan juice
6. Raise the temperature a little more to brown and remove when nice and golden brown

Freezing Instructions:

Cut chicken into large pieces and freeze in zip lock freezer bags or Tupperware for up to four months. Be sure and keep labels on hand so you can put the freeze date.

Cooking Directions:
Take meal out of the freezer the night before and leave it in the refrigerator all night. If not completely thawed by dinnertime take it out and let sit at room temperature for a little while. Reheat in roasting pan, under low to medium heat, the same way you cooked it the first time. Cover with tin foil.

Make this meal in bulk:
Makes three meals for a family of four

Ingredients measurements:

- 3 whole chickens
- 3 heads of garlic, peel all the cloves, chop coarsely
- 9 lemons, sliced, save a little lemon juice for later
- 3 tablespoons thyme
- 12 tablespoons olive oil
- Sea salt to taste
- Freshly ground black pepper to taste

Differences in Prep:
You will need three roasting pans.

Chicken with Almonds and Mango

Makes one meal for a family of four

Ingredients:

- 4 fillets of chicken breast, cubed.
- 1 cup diced mango
- 2 red onions, finely chopped
- 2 teaspoons coriander seeds
- 2 tablespoons soy sauce
- 4 tablespoons whole almonds
- Nuts and or pistachios (optional)
- Juice of 2 lemons
- 2 tablespoons coconut oil

Preparation Instructions:

1. Salt and pepper the chicken and set aside
2. Heat a skillet over medium heat, pour the coconut oil and let heat
3. Brown onion and coriander
4. Stir in the chicken and stir until cooked through
5. Add the soy sauce and let reduce
6. Stir in mango, almonds and dried fruit
7. Before serving, pour the juice of 1 lemon and stir again

Freezing Instructions:
Freeze in zip lock freezer bags or Tupperware for up to four months. Be sure and keep labels on hand so you can put the freeze date.

Cooking Directions:
Take the meal out of the freezer the night before and leave it in the refrigerator all night. If not completely thawed by

dinnertime take it out and let sit at room temperature for a little while. Reheat in skillet, the same way you cooked it the first time.

Make this meal in bulk:
Makes three meals for a family of four

Ingredients measurements:

- 12 fillets of chicken breast, cubed.
- 3 cup diced mango
- 6 red onions, finely chopped
- 6 teaspoons coriander seeds
- 6 tablespoons soy sauce
- 12 tablespoons whole almonds
- Nuts and or pistachios (optional)
- Juice of 6 lemons
- 6 tablespoons coconut oil

Differences in Prep:
Use a bigger pot or skillet (if you have one) or separate it and cook it in three portions.

Paleo People Eat *Meat* Dinners

Grilled Lamb Brochette with Mediterranean Salad

(If you freeze the lamb brochette, make the salad, and salad dressing fresh when you take the lamb out of the freezer)

Makes one meal for a family of four

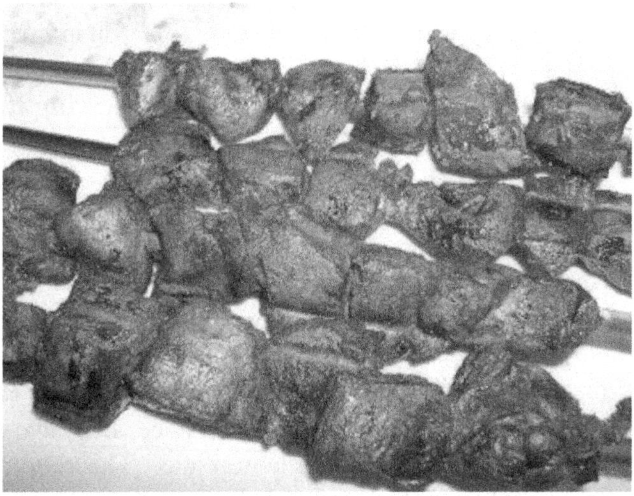

Ingredients:

- 1 lb. lamb (can substitute with beef if desired)
- 1 garlic clove, minced
- 4 tablespoons flat leaf parsley, chopped
- 1 cucumber, peeled and sliced thin
- 2 tomatoes
- 1 red onion
- 1 fennel, thinly sliced
- Dill
- Olive oil (2 parts)
- Juice of 1 lemon

- Mayonnaise

Preparation Instructions:

1. Cut Lamb into medium sized cubes
2. Marinate the lamb with the garlic, parsley, salt, pepper, and olive oil for at least an hour
3. Assemble the brochette with the lamb pieces and grill over hot coals to desired doneness (or broil in oven)

Salad (Prepare this when defrosting and serving the lamb-DO NOT FREEZE)

1. Cut the fennel and cucumber into thin slices
2. Cut the red onion in very thin slices
3. Cut the tomato into thin slices
4. Mix everything in a bowl along with the finely chopped dill
5. Dress the salad with the homemade mayonnaise, sea salt, freshly ground pepper, lemon juice, and olive oil. Three parts oil to one part lemon juice. This ratio of oil to acid is used in most salad dressings and a good general rule for any salad dressing you are making

Freezing Instructions:
Freeze in zip lock freezer bags or Tupperware for up to two to three months. Be sure and keep labels on hand so you can put the freeze date.

Cooking Directions:
Take the meal out of the freezer the night before and leave it in the refrigerator all night. If not completely thawed by dinnertime take it out and let sit at room temperature for a little while. Reheat in pan, or eat at room temperature (it's yummy both ways!). Prepare the salad

Make this meal in bulk:
Makes three meals for four people

Ingredients measurements:

- 3 lb. lamb (or beef)
- 3 garlic cloves, minced
- 12 tablespoons flat leaf parsley, chopped
- Salad would be the same as it would not be in bulk and will be prepared upon serving.

Differences in Prep:
Take the meal out of the freezer the night before and leave it in the refrigerator all night. If not completely thawed by dinnertime take it out and let sit at room temperature for a little while. Reheat in skillet, the same way you cooked it the first time.

Tenderloin Casserole with White Wine and Baked Vegetables

Makes one meal for a family of four

Ingredients:

- Tenderloin steaks, about 2 lbs.
- 6 medium onions cut into quarters
- 4 cloves of garlic, chopped finely
- Two handfuls of chopped flat leaf parsley
- 2 glasses of white wine

Preparation Instructions:

1. Cook onions in a saucepan until transparent
2. Add the garlic
3. Place tenderloin steaks on top and brown
4. Add white wine and cook for 10 min. longer
5. Cut the tenderloin into strips and cook for 5 minutes more
6. Serve hot
7. Side dish recommended "Roasted Vegetables" or "Mushrooms Provencal" (see recipe)

Freezing Instructions:
Freeze in zip lock freezer bags or Tupperware for up to two to three months. Be sure and keep labels on hand so you can put the freeze date.

Cooking Directions:
Take meal out of the freezer the night before and leave it in the refrigerator all night. If not completely thawed by dinnertime take it out and let sit at room temperature for a little while. Reheat in pan, the same way you cooked it the first time.

Make this meal in bulk:
Makes three meals for a family of four

Ingredients measurements:

- Tenderloin steaks, about 6 lbs
- 18 medium onions cut into quarters
- 12 cloves of garlic, chopped finely
- 6 handfuls of chopped flat leaf parsley
- 6 glasses of white wine

Differences in Prep:
Use a bigger pot vs. a pan (if you have one) or separate it and cook it in three portions.

Meat Balls

Makes one meal for a family of four

Ingredients:

- 3 lbs. of lean ground meat (you can use all one meat or a combination – I like to use about a pound each of beef, pork, and veal – sausage is good too as a substitute)
- 2 medium onion, finely chopped
- 2 tablespoons coconut oil
- 3 eggs
- ½ teaspoon pepper
- ¾ teaspoon nutmeg
- ½ teaspoon cayenne pepper

Sauce Ingredients:

- 2 cup beef or chicken broth
- 1 tablespoon of coconut oil

Preparation Instructions:

1. Heat a skillet over medium heat and add oil and onion. Sauté until fully cooked (10 min)
2. Preheat oven to 390 F.
3. Cover a baking sheet with parchment paper
4. Mix cooked onions and remaining meatball ingredients in a large bowl
5. Once mixed start forming the mixture into balls and place on the prepared baking sheet (20 meatballs)
6. Cook in the oven for 20 minutes

For the sauce:

1. Over low heat, put the broth in the pan with the oil
2. Leave a few minutes to reduce
3. Put the meatballs in a skillet and cover them with the reduced sauce and sauté for a few minutes. If there are any juices left in the tray where you cooked them, add those as well
4. Serve with "Sautéed Mushrooms" (see recipe)

Freezing Instructions:
Freeze in zip lock freezer bags or Tupperware for up to two to three months. Be sure and keep labels on hand so you can put the freeze date.

Cooking Directions:
Take meal out of the freezer the night before and leave it in the refrigerator all night. If not completely thawed by dinnertime take it out and let sit at room temperature for a little while. Reheat in oven, the same way you cooked it the first time but at a lower temperature.
Make this meal in bulk:
Makes three meals for a family of four

Ingredients measurements:

- 10 lbs. of lean ground meat
- 6 medium onion, finely chopped
- 6 tablespoon coconut oil
- 9 eggs
- 1 ½ teaspoon pepper
- 3 teaspoon nutmeg
- 1 ½ teaspoon cayenne pepper

Ingredients (sauce):

- 6 cup beef or chicken broth
- 3 tablespoon of coconut oil

Differences in Prep:
You will need three oven pans and depending on your oven size, you may have to cook them separately.

Wild Game Stew

Makes one meal for a family of four

Ingredients:

- 2 lbs. meat, chopped into nice sized chunks (you can use rabbit, venison, wild boar, or even beef or pork shoulder if none of the others are easily at hand)
- 5 large onions, sliced very thinly into feathers
- 3 tomatoes, peeled, seeded, and chopped
- 5 garlic cloves
- Juice of 1 lemon
- 1 glass of white wine
- Paprika to taste
- Freshly ground black pepper to taste
- Powdered thyme to taste
- 3 bay leaves
- 10 toasted almonds
- 2 Tablespoons coconut oil

Preparation Instructions:

1. In a pan, add a little coconut oil and garlic, cook until browned being careful not to burn the garlic
2. Add the chopped meat to the pan
3. Add the tomatoes, paprika, pepper, bay leaves and sauté
4. Add the onions
5. Lower heat and cook until reduced, adding lemon juice and the glass of white wine
6. Stir occasionally while the meat is cooking and the sauce is reducing
7. Grind the almonds in a mortar with a little raw garlic to make a paste

8. Continue to cook over low heat for about an hour and then remove coating with the almond garlic paste. Sprinkle a little thyme and sea salt on top and serve

Freezing Instructions:
Freeze in zip lock freezer bags or Tupperware for up to four to six months. Be sure and keep labels on hand so you can put the freeze date.

Cooking Directions:
Take meal out of the freezer the night before and leave it in the refrigerator all night. If not completely thawed by dinnertime take it out and let sit at room temperature for a little while. Reheat in pan, the same way you cooked it the first time.

Make this meal in bulk:
Makes three meals for a family of four

Ingredients measurements:

- 6 lbs. meat, chopped into nice sized chunks
- 15 large onions, sliced very thinly into feathers
- 9 tomatoes, peeled, seeded, and chopped
- 15 garlic cloves
- Juice of 3 lemons
- 3 glasses of white wine
- Paprika to taste
- Freshly ground black pepper to taste
- Powdered thyme to taste
- 9 bay leaves
- 30 toasted almonds
- 6 tablespoons coconut oil

Differences in Prep:
Use a huge pot if you have one, if not several pans.

Liver and Onions

Makes one meal for a family of four

Ingredients:

- 2 ¼ lbs. lamb's liver.
- Cayenne pepper
- 2 medium onions
- 2 bay leafs
- 2 tablespoons coconut oil
- Pinch of freshly ground black pepper
- Sea salt to taste

Preparation Instructions:

1. Clean the liver
2. Then cut it into thin slices and add a pinch of black pepper.
3. In a skillet, cook the finely chopped onion and bay leafs in coconut oil until the onions are transparent
4. Add the liver and cook for ten minutes over medium heat until browned
5. Then add the paprika and a dash of water
6. Cook until the liver is tender
7. Serve immediately

Freezing Instructions:

Freeze in zip lock freezer bags or Tupperware for up to two months. Be sure and keep labels on hand so you can put the freeze date.

Cooking Directions:

Take meal out of the freezer the night before and leave it in the refrigerator all night. If not completely thawed by dinnertime take it out and let sit at room temperature for a little while. Reheat in pan, the same way you cooked it the first time.

Make this meal in bulk:
Makes three meals for a family of four

Ingredients measurements:

- 6.5 lbs. lamb's liver.
- Cayenne pepper to taste
- 6 medium onions
- 6 bay leafs
- 6 tablespoons coconut oil
- Pinch of freshly ground black pepper to taste
- Sea salt to taste

Differences in Prep:
Use extra-large skillets; you may need two or three.

Lamb Casserole

Makes one meal for a family of four

Ingredients:

- 2 ¼ lbs. of lamb
- 2 large onions, sliced in quarters
- 4 cloves of garlic, minced
- 2 zucchinis, sliced
- 1 butternut squash, skin removed cubed into medium sized cubes
- 5 ripe tomatoes, cubed into medium sized cubes
- 2 glasses of white wine
- 4 sprigs of fresh cilantro for garnish
- 2 tablespoons extra virgin olive oil
- 1 cup of vegetable stock
- Cayenne pepper to taste
- 1 tiny portion of saffron
- Sea salt to taste

Preparation Instructions:

1. Marinate the lamb (between 30 and 60 minutes) in the fridge with garlic, paprika, saffron, olive oil and a sea salt
2. Boil butternut squash with a little salt until soft. Drain and set aside when ready.
3. Cook the chopped onion with a little oil in a saucepan until tender and transparent
4. Then add the chopped tomatoes and zucchini
5. When the vegetables are all cooked add a glass of wine and a cup of vegetable stock, cook on medium heat
6. When reduced (about 15-20 minutes), add the marinated tuna and simmer

7. When the tuna is done cooking add the cooked butternut squash
8. Turn off and let stand at least 20-30 minutes
9. Serve with a sprig of fresh cilantro on one side of the plate

Freezing Instructions:
Freeze in zip lock freezer bags or Tupperware for up to two to three months. Be sure and keep labels on hand so you can put the freeze date.

Cooking Directions:
Take meal out of the freezer the night before and leave it in the refrigerator all night. If not completely thawed by dinnertime take it out and let sit at room temperature for a little while. Reheat in pan, the same way you cooked it the first time.

Make this meal in bulk:
Makes three meals for a family of four

Ingredients measurements:

- 6 1/2 lbs. of lamb
- 6 large onions, sliced in quarters
- 12 cloves of garlic, minced
- 6 zucchinis, sliced
- 3 butternut squash, skin removed cubed into medium sized cubes
- 15 ripe tomatoes, cubed into medium sized cubes
- 3 glasses of white wine
- 4 sprigs of fresh cilantro for garnish
- 6 Tablespoons extra virgin olive oil
- 3 cup of vegetable stock
- Cayenne pepper to taste

- 3 tiny portions of saffron
- Sea salt to taste

Differences in Prep:
Heat in large pot or three large saucepans.

Dining on the Coasts - Seafood Dinners

Mussels Provencal

Makes one meal for a family of four

Ingredients:

- 4 ½ lbs. mussels in the shell (frozen is fine)
- 4 shallots, minced
- 2 glasses of white wine
- 1 lemon
- 3 garlic cloves, chopped finely
- 1 handful of flat leaf parsley, chopped finely
- Sea salt and freshly ground pepper to taste

Preparation Instructions:

1. Wash the mussels under running water and scrub them with a brush
2. In a large pot, add olive oil and sauté the minced shallot

3. When transparent add the mussels and white wine to the pot
4. Place over high heat and cover
5. Stir from time to time, until the mussels open and then leave them to cook a few minutes more with the lid on
6. Add the garlic and finely chopped parsley to the mussels
7. Add a squeeze of lemon juice if desired
8. (Do not eat any of the mussels that did not open during cooking)

Freezing Instructions:
Remove the meat from the mussel shells and freeze in Tupperware making sure they are covered with the broth. You can freeze for up to three or four months. Be sure and keep labels on hand so you can put the freeze date.

Cooking Directions:
Take meal out of the freezer the night before and leave it in the refrigerator all night. If not completely thawed by dinnertime take it out and let sit at room temperature for a little while. Reheat in pan, the same way you cooked it the first time.

Make this meal in bulk:
Makes three meals for a family of four

Ingredients measurements:

- 7 ½ lbs. mussels (in the shell)
- 12 shallots, minced
- 6 glasses of white wine
- 3 lemon
- 9 garlic cloves, chopped finely
- 3 handful of flat leaf parsley, chopped finely

- Sea salt and freshly ground pepper to taste

Differences in Prep:
Use a bigger pot vs. a pan (if you have one) or separate it and cook it in three portions.

Sautéed Shrimp with Asparagus

Makes one meal for a family of four

Ingredients:

- 2 lb. large shrimp
- 4 bunches asparagus, remove fibrous bases by bending until they break naturally, discard ends
- 2 onion, diced small
- 4 eggs, beaten
- 6 tablespoons extra virgin olive oil
- Sea salt to taste
- Freshly ground pepper to taste
- Red pepper flakes to taste

Preparation Instructions:

1. Add olive oil into the skillet
2. Heat the oil and add the onions
3. When the onions are transparent add the asparagus, and cook for 4 or 5 minutes more
4. Add salt, pepper, and red chili flakes to taste
5. Stir occasionally to prevent onions from burning
6. Remove from fire and put mixture into a separate plate and set aside
7. In the same pan add a little more olive oil and cook the previously cleaned prawns
8. When the shrimp are ready (they will be nice and pink and cook rather quickly), add the onions and asparagus back into the pan
9. Whisk eggs and add it to the mixture
10. Remove from heat and serve with a drizzle of extra virgin olive oil

Freezing Instructions:
Freeze in zip lock freezer bags or Tupperware for up to two months. Be sure and keep labels on hand so you can put the freeze date.

Cooking Directions:
Take meal out of the freezer the night before and leave it in the refrigerator all night. If not completely thawed by dinnertime take it out and let sit at room temperature for a little while. Reheat in pan, the same way you cooked it the first time.

Make this meal in bulk:
Makes three meals for a family of four

Ingredients measurements:

- 6 lbs. shrimp
- 12 bunches asparagus, remove fibrous bases by bending until they break naturally, discard ends
- 6 onion, diced small
- 12 eggs, beaten
- 18 tablespoons extra virgin olive oil
- Sea salt to taste
- Freshly ground pepper to taste
- Red pepper flakes to taste

Differences in Prep:
Use an extra large skillet or cook in three batches.

Galician Octopus

Makes one meal for a family of four

Ingredients:

- 2 octopus (~6 lbs.) [If you can't find these at your local seafood market they can be ordered from http://www.freshseafood.com/fresh-octopus-383.html or you can substitute squid or calamari]
- 8 medium sweet potatoes, boiled and sliced
- 2 onion, sliced
- 4 bay leaves
- Paprika to taste
- Extra virgin olive oil to taste

Preparation Instructions:

For the octopus, we have two possibilities. You can buy precooked octopus, which is easier because it only needs to be 5 min. in boiling water but if you buy one raw, the steps to prepare it are as follows:

1. It is best to freeze it before cooking because the muscle fibers break down and the flesh will be much tenderer when cooked. Once frozen for about 24 hours, put it in the fridge and let it thaw out there
2. Once thawed, clean it well, especially the head
3. Put into pot of boiling water with onion and bay leaves, turning it over occasionally
4. To make the octopus shrink properly, completely remove and submerge the octopus from the boiling water three times
5. Leave to cook. If the octopus is medium, half an hour will suffice, if large, a little longer
6. Now take it out and let it cool.

7. Cut the tentacles into slices and the head into medium sized pieces always checking to make sure it is very clean
8. On a large platter, make a layer of sweet potatoes, next make a layer of octopus and dress with the extra virgin olive oil and paprika. Optional, a little bit of sea salt and freshly ground pepper if you taste it and feel it needs it

Freezing Instructions:
Freeze in zip lock freezer bags or Tupperware for up to two to three months. Be sure and keep labels on hand so you can put the freeze date.

Cooking Directions:
Take meal out of the freezer the night before and leave it in the refrigerator all night. If not completely thawed by dinnertime take it out and let sit at room temperature for a little while. Reheat in large pot the same way you cooked it the first time.

Make this meal in bulk:
Makes three meals for a family of four

Ingredients measurements:

- 6 octopus (18 lbs.)
- 24 medium sweet potatoes, boiled and sliced
- 6 onion, sliced
- 4 bay leaves
- Paprika to taste
- Extra virgin olive oil to taste

\

Differences in Prep:
You will need two or three of the same size pot and cook separately.

Baked Fish

Makes one meal for a family of four

Ingredients:

- 4 fillets of fresh tuna or salmon
- 7 medium sweet potatoes, sliced
- 2 red pepper
- 2 onions, chopped
- 2 large tomatoes, sliced
- 4 cloves of garlic, minced
- 2 tablespoons olive oil
- Freshly ground pepper to taste
- Juice of one lemon
- Handful of chopped, fresh, flat leaf parsley

Preparation Instructions:

1. In a large skillet with a little oil in it, add the sweet potatoes, garlic, onions, and tomato and cook for a few minutes
2. When these ingredients are soft and cooked well with the onions transparent, put then into an oven pan with the slices of fish on top
3. Cook in the oven at 360 F for 30 minutes. When it is half way cooked add the lemon juice on top
4. Serve with chopped parsley and a drizzle of olive oil

Freezing Instructions:

Freeze in zip lock freezer bags or Tupperware for up to four to six months. Be sure and keep labels on hand so you can put the freeze date.

Cooking Directions:

Take meal out of the freezer the night before and leave it in the refrigerator all night. If not completely thawed by dinnertime take it out and let sit at room temperature for a little while. Reheat in pan, the same way you cooked it the first time.

Make this meal in bulk:
Makes three meals for a family of four

Ingredients measurements:

- 12 filets of fresh tuna or salmon
- 21 medium sweet potatoes, sliced
- 6 red pepper
- 6 onions, chopped
- 6 large tomatoes, sliced
- 12 cloves of garlic, minced
- 6 Tablespoons olive oil
- Freshly ground pepper to taste
- Juice of 3 lemons
- 1 handful of chopped, fresh, flat leaf parsley

Differences in Prep:
Use a bigger pot vs. a pan (if you have one) or separate it and cook it in three portions

Tuna Salad

Makes one meal for a family of four

Ingredients:

- 3 cans of tuna in water
- 1 onion, chopped finely
- 1 head of the lettuce of your choice (purchase within days of defrosting and serving.)
- 3 tablespoons lemon juice
- 3 tablespoons chopped cilantro
- 3 tablespoons extra virgin olive oil
- 2 avocados, sliced into thin slices (purchase within days of defrosting and serving.)
- Sea salt to taste
- Freshly ground black pepper to taste

Preparation Instructions:

Flake tuna and mix with onion, lemon juice, cilantro, oil, pepper and salt. Serve tuna on lettuce leaves and avocado.

Freezing Instructions:

Freeze tuna mixture in zip lock freezer bags or Tupperware for up three months. Be sure and keep labels on hand so you can put the freeze date. Lettuce and avocado must be used fresh and not frozen.

Make this meal in bulk:

Makes three meals for a family of four

Ingredients measurements:

- 9 cans of tuna in water
- 3 onion, chopped finely

- 3 head of the lettuce of your choice (purchase within days of defrosting and serving.)
- 9 tablespoons lemon juice
- 9 tablespoons chopped cilantro
- 9 tablespoons extra virgin olive oil
- 2 avocados, sliced into thin slices (purchase within days of defrosting and serving.)
- Sea salt to taste
- Freshly ground black pepper to taste

Differences in Prep:
Use extra-large bowls or a few large bowls.

Garlic Shrimp

Makes one meal for a family of four

Ingredients:

- 2 lbs. of cleaned and frozen shrimp (raw, thawed, and dried thoroughly with paper towels)
- 8 cloves of garlic, minced
- 4 hot chili peppers, chopped
- 2 tablespoons extra virgin olive oil
- 1 handful of fresh, flat leaf parsley, roughly chopped

Preparation Instructions:

1. In a large casserole dish add the oil and cook the garlic, chili peppers on medium heat
2. When the garlic is golden, add the shrimp and let cook about 3-5 minutes
3. Serve in the same casserole topped with parsley

Freezing Instructions:
Freeze in zip lock freezer bags or Tupperware for up to two months. Be sure and keep labels on hand so you can put the freeze date.

Cooking Directions:
Take meal out of the freezer the night before and leave it in the refrigerator all night. If not completely thawed by dinnertime take it out and let sit at room temperature for a little while. Reheat in casserole dish, the same way you cooked it the first time.

Make this meal in bulk:
Makes three meals for a family of four

Ingredients measurements:

- 6 ½ lbs. of cleaned and frozen shrimp or prawns (raw, thawed, and dried thoroughly with paper towels)
- 24 cloves of garlic, minced
- 12 hot chili peppers, chopped
- 6 Tablespoons extra virgin olive oil
- 1 handful of fresh, flat leaf parsley, roughly chopped

Differences in Prep:
Use three casserole dishes.

Veggie Dinners and Sides

Mushrooms Provencal

Makes one meal or 2 side dishes for a family of four

Ingredients:

- 2 ½ lbs. of mushrooms, washed, drained, and cut into quarters
- 2 cloves garlic, minced
- 1 small handful of chopped flat leaf parsley
- 1 tablespoon olive oil
- Sea salt to taste
- Freshly ground black pepper to taste

Preparation Instructions:

1. In a pan add olive oil, heat and then add the mushrooms
2. Move them to brown on all sides
3. When slightly browned add garlic and parsley and stir
4. Serve with a splash of olive oil, a light sprinkle of sea salt, and freshly ground pepper on top

Freezing Instructions:

Freeze in zip lock freezer bags or Tupperware for up to nine months. Be sure and keep labels on hand so you can put the freeze date.

Cooking Directions:
Take meal out of the freezer the night before and leave it in the refrigerator all night. If not completely thawed by dinnertime take it out and let sit at room temperature for a little while. Reheat in pan, the same way you cooked it the first time.

Make this meal in bulk:
Makes three meals for a family of four

Ingredients measurements:

- 5 ½ lbs. of mushrooms, washed, drained, and cut into quarters
- 6 cloves garlic, minced
- 3 small handful of chopped flat leaf parsley
- 3 Tablespoons olive oil
- Sea salt to taste
- Freshly ground black pepper to taste

Differences in Prep:
Use a bigger pan (if you have one) or separate it and cook it in three portions.

Scrambled Zucchini

Makes one meal for a family of four

Ingredients:

- 8 zucchinis, chopped
- 2 small onions, finely chopped
- 15 cherry tomatoes
- 16 basil leaves
- 4 slices of prosciutto, sliced into thin slices
- 4 eggs
- Sea salt to taste
- Freshly ground black pepper to taste
- 2 tablespoons extra virgin olive oil
- Cayenne pepper to taste

Preparation Instructions:

1. In a medium skillet, sauté the prosciutto in a little olive oil in a pan and set aside on a separate dish
2. In the same pan, brown the onions for 1 minute
3. Add zucchinis
4. Add salt and pepper
5. Cook for 2 minutes more
6. Add the cherry tomatoes and cook for another minute
7. Beat eggs and add to the preparation stirring to integrate the egg preparation
8. Serve with a drizzle of extra virgin olive oil on top with a little salt, pepper and the prosciutto chips

Freezing Instructions:
Freeze in zip lock freezer bags or Tupperware for up to two months. Be sure and keep labels on hand so you can put the freeze date.

Cooking Directions:
Take meal out of the freezer the night before and leave it in the refrigerator all night. If not completely thawed by dinnertime take it out and let sit at room temperature for a little while. Reheat in pan, the same way you cooked it the first time.

Make this meal in bulk:
Makes three meals for a family of four

Ingredients measurements:

- 24 zucchinis, chopped
- 6 small onions, finely chopped
- 45 cherry tomatoes
- 48 basil leaves
- 12 slices of prosciutto, sliced into thin slices
- 12 Eggs
- Sea salt to taste
- Freshly ground black pepper to taste
- 6 Tablespoons extra virgin olive oil
- Cayenne pepper to taste

Differences in Prep:
Use a bigger pan (if you have one) or separate it and cook it in three portions.

Zucchini Omelets and Tomato Salad

Makes one meal or 2 side-dishes for a family of four

Ingredients:

- 2 yellow onions, chopped
- 2 cloves of garlic
- 2 zucchinis, sliced
- 8 eggs, beaten
- Tomato cut into wedges
- Red onion, cut in thin feather like slices
- 1 tablespoons olive oil
- 1 tablespoons extra virgin olive oil
- Dried oregano to taste
- Sea salt to taste
- Freshly ground black pepper to taste

Preparation Instructions:

1. In a pan, heat olive oil and add the onion and zucchini
2. Brown and then add a little salt and pepper
3. When the zucchini gets soft add eggs
4. Cook for 5 minutes and flip the omelet, cooking the other side until the desired doneness. We all have different tastes regarding this
5. For the salad mix in separate bowl the tomatoes, red onion, and season with oregano, extra virgin olive oil, vinegar, salt and pepper

Freezing Instructions:

Freeze in zip lock freezer bags or Tupperware for up to 6 months. Be sure and keep labels on hand so you can put the freeze date. Make the salad fresh, as it cannot be frozen.

Cooking Directions:
Take meal out of the freezer the night before and leave it in the refrigerator all night. If not completely thawed by dinnertime take it out and let sit at room temperature for a little while. Reheat in pan, the same way you cooked it the first time.

Make this meal in bulk:
Makes three meals for four people

Ingredients measurements:

- 6 yellow onions, chopped
- 6 cloves of garlic
- 6 zucchinis, sliced
- 28 eggs, beaten
- 3 tomatoes cut into wedges
- 3 red onions, cut in thin feather like slices
- 3 tablespoons olive oil
- 1 tablespoons extra virgin olive oil
- Dried oregano to taste
- Sea salt to taste
- Freshly ground black pepper to taste

Differences in Prep:
Use a bigger pan (if you have one) or separate it and cook it in three portions.

Stuffed Avocado

Makes one meal for a family of four

Ingredients:

- 2 lbs. lobster (may substitute with shrimp), boiled and drained

The remaining ingredients are made fresh when defrosting the lobster and serving.

- 8 avocados, cut in half, remove the seeds. Remove a little of the avocado flesh to make the pit large enough to fit the filling. Leave the skin on.
- 5 medium sized ripe tomatoes, chopped into small pieces
- 16 asparagus, blanched, and chopped into small pieces
- 2 eggs
- 2 cloves of garlic
- 1 cup extra virgin olive oil
- 4 tablespoons fresh dill, finely chopped (save a few sprigs for garnish after)
- Sea salt to taste
- Freshly ground pepper to taste
- Cayenne pepper to taste

Preparation Instructions:

1. Boil the lobster or shrimp. Drain and reserve in the fridge.
2. With a hand mixer we will prepare a mayonnaise with the garlic, salt, and egg

3. Continue mixing with the mixer while adding the extra virgin olive oil until you have a mayonnaise consistency, this is your homemade mayo
4. In a blender, blend the dill and olive oil
5. Fill avocados with tomatoes and asparagus.
6. Top with homemade mayonnaise
7. Garnish with a sprig of fresh dill and a little of the dill oil over the top

Freezing Instructions:
Freeze lobster or shrimp in zip lock freezer bags or Tupperware for up to two months. Be sure and keep labels on hand so you can put the freeze date. The rest of the recipe is made fresh.

Cooking Directions:
Take lobster or shrimp out of the freezer the night before and leave it in the refrigerator all night. If not completely thawed by dinner time take it out and let sit at room temperature for a little while. Follow cooking instructions for making it fresh.

Make this meal in bulk:
Makes three meals for a family of four

Ingredients measurements:

- 6 Lbs. lobster (or shrimp), boiled and drained

Differences in Prep:
Use a bigger pot (if you have one) or separate it and cook it in three portions.

Spinach with Coconut and Spices

Makes one side-dish for a family of four

Ingredients:

- 2 shallots
- 2 cloves of garlic
- Sea salt to taste
- 2 tablespoons of coconut oil
- ½ teaspoon yellow mustard seeds
- ½ teaspoon cumin seeds
- ½ teaspoon cayenne pepper
- 2 cups thinly sliced asparagus
- 1 lb. of spinach, washed thoroughly and chopped
- Juice of 1 lemon
- 3 tablespoons lightly toasted grated coconut

Preparation Instructions:

1. Place the shallot and garlic in a mortar with a little salt and make a thick paste.
2. Heat the oil in a skillet over medium heat. Add the seeds and cover the pan with a lid. Leave them until toasted. Careful not to burn
3. Then add the cayenne pepper. Let cook for another minute
4. Add the asparagus and cook for one minute more
5. Then add the spinach
6. Stir ingredients until the spinach begins to cook (about 1 minute).
7. Finish my garnishing with a little lemon juice and some of the toasted, grated coconut

Freezing Instructions:
Freeze in zip lock freezer bags or Tupperware for up to nine months. Be sure and keep labels on hand so you can put the freeze date.

Cooking Directions:
Take meal out of the freezer the night before and leave it in the refrigerator all night. If not completely thawed by dinnertime take it out and let sit at room temperature for a little while. Reheat in skillet, the same way you cooked it the first time.

Make this meal in bulk:
Makes three side-dishes for a family of four

Ingredients measurements:

- 6 shallots
- 6 cloves of garlic
- Sea salt to taste
- 6 tablespoons of coconut oil
- 1 ½ teaspoon yellow mustard seeds
- 1 ½ teaspoon cumin seeds
- 1 ½ teaspoon cayenne pepper
- 6 cups thinly sliced asparagus
- 3 lbs. of spinach, washed thoroughly and chopped
- Juice of 3 lemons
- 9 tablespoons lightly toasted grated coconut

Differences in Prep:
Use a bigger skillet (if you have one) or separate it and cook it in three portions.

Artichoke Omelets

Makes one meal for a family of four

Ingredients:

- 2 trays of artichoke hearts, chopped
- 2 large leeks
- 8 free-range eggs, beaten
- 2 tablespoons extra virgin olive oil
- Sea salt to taste
- Freshly ground black pepper to taste

Preparation Instructions:

1. Cut the leeks into rings and sauté in olive oil for 3 minutes
2. In a medium bowl combine the beaten eggs, artichokes, leeks, and a pinch of salt
3. Heat a little oil in a pan and pour the mixture in, letting it simmer
4. Cook on both sides until desired doneness is achieved

Freezing Instructions:
Freeze in zip lock freezer bags or Tupperware for up to two to three months. Be sure and keep labels on hand so you can put the freeze date.

Cooking Directions:
Take meal out of the freezer the night before and leave it in the refrigerator all night. If not completely thawed by dinnertime take it out and let sit at room temperature for a little while. Reheat in pan, the same way you cooked it the first time.

Make this meal in bulk:
Makes three meals for a family of four

Ingredients measurements:

- 6 trays of artichoke hearts, chopped
- 6 large leeks
- 24 free-range eggs, beaten
- 6 tablespoons extra virgin olive oil
- Sea salt to taste
- Freshly ground black pepper to taste

Differences in Prep:
Use a bigger pan (if you have one) or separate it and cook it in three portions.

Conclusion

Thank you again for purchasing this book!

I hope it was able to help you stock your freezer with some delicious and nutritious Paleo meals, without the hassle of cooking for hours each night.

The next step is to memorize your favorites, so you can whip them up quickly on a regular basis. Also experiment further by tweaking the recipes to make them your own. Get creative!

Finally, if you enjoyed this book, please take the time to share your thoughts and post a review on Amazon. It'd be greatly appreciated!

Thank you and good luck!

Lucy

Check out the other Yummy books in my Paleo Diet Solution Series!!

http://www.amazon.com/dp/B00HH1GBLC

http://www.amazon.com/dp/B00HH1GFRC

Made in the USA
Monee, IL
19 October 2026

66035039R00036